JUAN RAMÓN JIMÉNEZ

Selected Poems

JUAN RAMÓN JIMÉNEZ
Selected Poems

Edited and Translated
by

Salvador Ortiz-Carboneres

Aris & Phillips is an imprint of Oxbow Books

Published in the United Kingdom by
OXBOW BOOKS
10 Hythe Bridge Street, Oxford OX1 2EW

and in the United States by
OXBOW BOOKS
908 Darby Road, Havertown, PA 19083

Paperback Edition: ISBN 978-0-85668-760-0

First printed 2006
Paperback reprint 2014

A CIP record for this book is available from the British Library

For a complete list of Aris & Phillips titles, please contact:

UNITED KINGDOM
Oxbow Books
Telephone (01865) 241249
Fax (01865) 794449
Email: oxbow@oxbowbooks.com
www.oxbowbooks.com

UNITED STATES OF AMERICA
Oxbow Books
Telephone (800) 791-9354
Fax (610) 853-9146
Email: queries@casemateacademic.com
www.casemateacademic.com/oxbow

Oxbow Books is part of the Casemate Group
Printed and bound by CPI Group (UK) Ltd, Croydon, CR0 4YY

FSC
www.fsc.org

MIX
Paper from
responsible sources
FSC® C013604

To my dear friend
Trudie Berger

CONTENTS

ACKNOWLEDGEMENTS

I would like to thank all my friends and colleagues who have helped me to make this translation possible. I am particularly grateful to Professor Eric Hawkins and Ms Athena Economides who helped me to render an accurate English version of the original text. I am also indebted to Professor Susan Bassnett for her invaluable advice and for the preface in this book. My thanks also go to Miss Sam Black and Mrs Anne Lakey who have given tireless secretarial assistance and have greatly helped me to bring this project to completion. Finally, my thanks and gratitude to Doña Carmen Hernández–Pinzón Moreno and the Heirs of Don Juan Ramón Jiménez, copyright holders, who have granted their permission for the publication of this translation with their Spanish originals and also for the photographs in this publication.

PREFACE

Juan Ramón Jiménez, who was awarded the Nobel Prize for Literature in 1956, is not as well-known in the English-speaking world as he deserves to be. This translation of a selection of his verse, from an early collection published in 1911 through to poems published much later in his life, offers readers an opportunity to catch a sense of his extraordinary linguistic talent and his ability to transform the everyday into something that is both magical and mystical. Jiménez was a transcendental poet, a writer whose sense of empathy with the natural world combined with a capacity for observation that enabled him to write poems of exquisite detail.

He was a prolific writer, whose collected poetry fills twenty volumes, and who published his first verses when still in his teens. Born in 1881, in Moguer, a small Andalucian town, to a middle-class family, he seemed destined to become a lawyer, but the death of his father in 1900 proved so traumatic that he abandoned his studies and, for a time, shut himself away in Moguer. Throughout his life, Jiménez was to suffer fragile mental health, with a tendency to depression. After the death of his beloved wife, Zenobia, in 1956, just three days after hearing that he had been awarded the Nobel Prize, Jiménez again withdrew from the world, and died not long afterwards in May, 1958.

Despite his melancholic temperament and his spells of hospitalization for depression, Jiménez was a man committed to poetry and to ideals of human liberty. He was very active in literary circles in the first three decades of the twentieth century, encouraging many writers from Spain and Latin America. When the Civil War broke out he supported the Republican cause, and chose exile in 1939, shortly before Franco's forces crushed the opposition. He stayed in the United States, pursuing a successful academic career in various cities, and travelled extensively throughout Latin America, spending time in Cuba and Puerto Rico, where he and his wife eventually settled. After his death, his remains were brought back to Spain, and the bodies of Jiménez and his Zenobia lie in the soil of his native Moguer.

Jiménez is a difficult poet to label: he had strong affiliations with *modernismo*, and greatly admired Rubén Darío – a mutual admiration, for Darío published a collection of poems in 1923 dedicated to Jiménez. English readers may find hints in his poetry that remind them of García Lorca also, but there is a powerful mystical strain in his writing that can be traced back to the great Spanish poets of the high Renaissance, such as Saint John of the Cross. Like the earlier mystics, Jiménez wrestled with his inner self and sought to express his struggle in poetry. His poem 'Sea' transposes that inner struggle into the wild movement of waves, as the sea wrestles with 'endless disorder' and loneliness. In 'Nocturne', a poem dedicated to Antonio Machado, another poet greatly admired by Jiménez, he looks up at the vastness of the heavens and hears 'a piercing cry, immense and lonely, /like a wandering star'. In 'Memories', the poet laments that even the stars deceive him. Keywords in his poetry include *nada* (nothingness) *estrella* (star) *fondo* (depths) *sombra* (shadow) *sueño* (dream), words that summon up stillness, absence or silence; but in contrast, key images that recur in his poems are all about motion, such as running water, the movement of waves, wind and stars, the flight of birds, flowers that open in sunlight.

'October' is a poem in which many different aspects of Jiménez' poetry come together. This sonnet is full of powerful feeling, stirred by watching the movement of a plough in a field somewhere in Castile. The poet observes the plough carving through the soil, watches the ensuing sowing of seeds in the furrows and fantasizes about throwing his own heart, with its 'deep, lofty feelings' (the contradiction between height and depth is deliberate) into the broad furrow of his native land to see what might grow the following Spring. What startles about this poem is its sensuality, that combines with profound spirituality and close observation of a simple, peasant activity; and the poet's use of the adverb *honradamente,* which the translator has rendered as 'chastely', draws our attention to the physicality of ploughing, the moment of man's intercourse with nature that is, nevertheless, chastely performed.

Jiménez' great skill is in his sparing use of words. Some of his poems are tiny, not more than two or three lines that still contain all that the poet needs to say. The translator has striven to offer English-language readers a sense of the power Jiménez put into his poetry, adhering to his structures, yet endeavouring not to distort the English, for beauty through simplicity was Jiménez' goal. My favourite lines in this collection, from 'Yellow Spring', manage to echo the Spanish, yet can stand on their own in English, a fitting epitaph to one of Europe's greatest twentieth-century poets:

> Among the bones of the dead
> God was opening his yellow hands.

Susan Bassnett, University of Warwick, April 2004

Poemas Májicos y Dolientes
(1911)

Poemas Agrestes
(1910–1911)

La Frente Pensativa
(1911–1912)

PRIMAVERA AMARILLA

Abril venía, lleno
todo de flores amarillas:
amarillo el arroyo,

amarillo el vallado, la colina,
el cementerio de los niños,
el huerto aquel donde el amor vivía.

El sol unjía de amarillo el mundo,
con sus luces caídas;
¡ay, por los lirios áureos,
el agua de oro, tibia;
las amarillas mariposas
sobre las rosas amarillas!

Guirnaldas amarillas escalaban
los árboles: el día
era una gracia perfumada de oro,
en un dorado despertar de vida.
Entre los huesos de los muertos
abría Dios sus manos amarillas.

Poemas májicos y dolientes

YELLOW SPRING

April was coming, brimming
with yellow flowers:
the brook ran yellow,

and yellow were the fence and the hill,
the graveyard of the children,
and the orchard where love dwelt.

The sun was anointing the world with yellow,
in a shower of sun beams;
through the golden lilies,
the warm sparkling water;
the yellow butterflies
over the yellow roses.

Yellow garlands were growing
up the trees; the day
was a blessing of golden incense
in a sunny awakening of life.
Among the bones of the dead,
God was opening his yellow hands.

EL VIAJE DEFINITIVO

…Y yo me iré. Y se quedarán los pájaros cantando;
y se quedará mi huerto con su verde árbol
y con su pozo blanco.

Todas las tardes, el cielo será azul y plácido;
y tocarán, como esta tarde están tocando,
las campanas del campanario.

Se morirán aquéllos que me amaron;
y el pueblo se hará nuevo cada año;
y en el rincón aquel de mi huerto florido y encalado,
mi espíritu errará, nostáljico…

Y yo me iré; y estaré solo, sin hogar, sin árbol
verde, sin pozo blanco,
sin cielo azul y plácido…
Y se quedarán los pájaros cantando.

Poemas agrestes

4

THE FINAL JOURNEY

...And I shall leave. And the birds will remain, still singing;
my garden will remain, with its green tree,
and its white well.

Every afternoon, the sky will be tranquil and blue;
the bells will ring in the belfry,
just as they do this afternoon.

And those, who once loved me, will die;
the town will renew itself each year;
and in a corner of my white-walled garden in full bloom,
my spirit will wander, nostalgically...

...And I shall leave; I shall be alone, homeless,
without a green tree, or a white well,
nor a peaceful blue sky...
And the birds will remain, still singing.

AMOR

No has muerto, no.
                    Renaces,
con las rosas, en cada primavera.
    Como la vida, tienes
tus hojas secas;
tienes tu nieve, como
la vida...
            Mas tu tierra
amor, está sembrada
de profundas promesas,
que han de cumplirse aun en el mismo
olvido.
    ¡En vano es que no quieras!
La brisa dulce torna, un día, al alma;
una noche de estrellas,
bajas, amor, a los sentidos,
casto como la vez primera.
    ¡Pues eres puro, eres
eterno! A tu presencia,
vuelven por el azul, en blanco bando,
tiernas palomas que creímos muertas...
Abres la sola flor con nuevas hojas....
Doras la inmortal luz con lenguas nuevas...
    ¡Eres eterno, amor,
como la primavera!

La frente pensativa

LOVE

You are not dead, no.
                    You are reborn,
with the roses, every spring.
Like life, you have
your dry leaves;
you have your snow,
like life…
  But your soil,
love, is sown
with deep promises,
which must be fulfilled, even
in oblivion.
  Your desire not to love is in vain!
The fresh breeze will return one day to your soul;
love, you pull the heart strings,
a night of stars,
chaste as the first time.
  Since you are pure, you are
eternal! Through the blue,
the gentle doves we thought dead,
fly back to you in a white flock…
You open every single flower with new leaves…
You gild the immortal light with new tongues…
  Love, you are eternal,
like the spring!

Sonetos Espirituales
(1914–1915)

Diario de un Poeta
Recién Casado
(1916)

OCTUBRE

Estaba echado yo en la tierra, enfrente
del infinito campo de Castilla,
que el otoño envolvía en la amarilla
dulzura de su claro sol poniente.

Lento, el arado, paralelamente
abría el haza oscura, y la sencilla
mano abierta dejaba la semilla
en su entraña partida honradamente.

Pensé arrancarme el corazón, y echarlo,
pleno de su sentir alto y profundo,
al ancho surco del terruño tierno,

a ver si con partirlo y con sembrarlo,
la primavera le mostraba al mundo
el árbol puro del amor eterno.

Sonetos espirituales

OCTOBER

I was lying down on the ground, in front of
the infinite countryside of Castile,
while autumn was bathing the fields in the yellow
sweetness of its clear sunset.

Slowly, the plough spread apart,
in parallel tracks, the dark soil and an open
rural hand began to scatter the seed
in its chastely broken open depths.

I thought of wrenching out my heart and tossing it
full of its lofty deep feelings,
in the broad furrow of my tender native land,

to see if, by shredding it and sowing it,
spring would reveal to the world
the chaste tree of eternal love.

A MI ALMA

Siempre tienes la rama preparada
para la rosa justa; andas alerta
siempre, el oído cálido en la puerta
de tu cuerpo, a la flecha inesperada.

Una onda no pasa de la nada,
que no se lleve de tu sombra abierta
la luz mejor. De noche, estás despierta
en tu estrella, a la vida desvelada.

Signo indeleble pones en las cosas.
Luego, tornada gloria de las cumbres,
revivirás en todo lo que sellas.

Tu rosa será norma de las rosas,
tu oír de la armonía, de las lumbres
tu pensar, tu velar de las estrellas.

Sonetos espirituales

12

TO MY SOUL

Day after day you keep the branch waiting
in case the right rose comes; you are always
alert, your welcoming ear at the gateway
of your body, awaiting the unforeseen arrow.

No wave emerges out of nothingness,
it carries with it the best light
of your free shadow. At night, you are awake
within your star, to wakeful life.

On all things you leave a permanent mark;
then, after embodying the glory of the summits,
you will revive all that which you anoint.

Your rose will be the pattern of all roses;
your ear, of harmony; your thought of light,
and your wakefulness the pattern of the stars.

Madrid

17 de enero de 1916

    ¡Qué cerca ya del alma
lo que está tan inmensamente lejos
de las manos aún!

        Como una luz de estrella,
como una voz sin nombre
traída por el sueño, como el paso
de algún corcel remoto
que oímos, anhelantes,
el oído en la tierra;
como el mar en teléfono…

    Y se hace la vida
por dentro, con la luz inestinguible
de un día deleitoso
que brilla en otra parte.

    ¡Oh, qué dulce, qué dulce
verdad sin realidad aún, qué dulce!

Diario de un poeta recién casado

Madrid

January, 17, 1916

How close to my soul now
something which is still so immensely far
from our reach!

Like the light of a star,
like a nameless voice
heard in a dream, like the passing
of some distant steed
we long to hear
with our ear close to the ground,
like the sea over a telephone line...

And life is born
within us, with the inextinguishable light
of an enchanting day
shining elsewhere.

Oh, how sweet, how sweet,
truth not realised yet, how sweet!

MAR

Parece, mar, que luchas
– ¡oh desorden sin fin, hierro incesante! –
por encontrarte o porque yo te encuentre.
¡Qué inmenso demostrarte,
en tu desnudez sola
– sin compañera… o sin compañero,
según te diga el mar o la mar –, creando
el espectáculo completo
de nuestro mundo de hoy!
Estás, como en un parto,
dándote a luz – ¡con qué fatiga! –
a ti mismo, ¡mar único!,
a ti mismo, a ti solo y en tu misma
y sola plenitud de plenitudes,
…¡por encontrarte o porque yo te encuentre!

Diario de un poeta recién casado

SEA

It seems, sea, that you are struggling,
– oh endless disorder, unceasing weapon! –
seeking yourself only for me to find you.
What immense unfolding,
in your lonely nakedness
– with neither man nor woman as companion…
according to which I call you he or she,
creating the whole image
of our world today!
You are bringing yourself into the world,
giving birth – gasping for breath! –
into yourself, singular sea!
to yourself alone, in your own
unique fullness of fullnesses,
seeking yourself only for me to find you!

CIELO

Te tenía olvidado,
cielo, y no eras
más que un vago esistir de luz,
visto – sin nombre –
por mis cansados ojos indolentes.
Y aparecías, entre las palabras
perezosas y desesperanzadas del viajero,
como en breves lagunas repetidas
de un paisaje de agua visto en sueños...

Hoy te he mirado lentamente,
y te has ido elevando hasta tu nombre.

Diario de un poeta recién casado

SKY

I had forgotten you,
sky, and you were no more
than a vague presence of light,
seen – unknown –
by my wearied, indolent eyes.
And you appeared, among the idle
and hopeless words of the traveller,
as a vision of brief repeated lagoons
in a watery landscape seen in dreams…

Today I have gazed at you slowly
and you have been living up to your name.

NOCTURNO

(A ANTONIO MACHADO)

..Es la celeste jeometría
de un astrónomo viejo
sobre la ciudad alta – torres
negras, finas, pequeñas, fin de aquello...–

Como si, de un mirador último,
lo estuviera mirando
el astrólogo.

   Signos
esactos – fuegos y colores –
con su secreto bajo y desprendido
en diáfana atmósfera
de azul y honda trasparencia.

¡Qué brillos, qué amenazas,
qué fijezas, qué augurios,
en la inminencia cierta
de la estraña verdad! ¡Anatomía
del cielo, con la ciencia
de la función en sí y para nosotros!

– Un grito agudo, inmenso y solo,
como una estrella errante –.
     ...¡Cuán lejanos
ya de aquellos nosotros,
de aquella primavera de ayer tarde
– en Washington Square, tranquila y dulce –
de aquellos sueños y de aquel amor!

Diario de un poeta recién casado

NOCTURNE

(To ANTONIO MACHADO)

...It is the celestial geometry
of an old astronomer
overlooking the tall city – black-lined towers,
slender, small, the far end of all that ...

As if, from an ultimate observatory,
the astrologer
were observing it all.

       Signs
pure signs – fires and colours –
with their subtle secret released
in the diaphanous atmosphere
of a deep blue transparency.

What brightness, what menace,
what insistence, what omens
in the definite imminence
of a strange truth! Anatomy
of the sky, of the science
of its movement within itself and for us!

A piercing cry, immense and lonely,
like a wondering star –
         ...How remote now,
from what we once were,
from that springtime on that afternoon
– tranquil and pleasant Washington Square –
from those dreams, and from that love!

Eternidades
(1916–1917)

¡Intelijencia, dame
el nombre esacto de las cosas!
     …Que mi palabra sea
la cosa misma,
creada por mi alma nuevamente.
Que por mí vayan todos
los que no las conocen, a las cosas;
que por mí vayan todos
los que ya las olvidan, a las cosas;
que por mí vayan todos
los mismos que las aman, a las cosas…
¡Intelijencia, dame
el nombre esacto, y tuyo,
y suyo, y mío, de las cosas!

                              Eternidades

Intelligence, oh give me
the precise name of things!
... So that my word might be
the thing in itself,
newly created by my soul.
Let those who have no knowledge
of things, reach them through me;
through me, may all those,
who forget things reach them;
even those who love things,
let them approach them through me...
Intelligence, oh give me
the precise name, and your name
and theirs, and mine, for all things!

Vino, primero, pura,
vestida de inocencia.
Y la amé como un niño.

Luego se fue vistiendo
de no sé qué ropajes.
Y la fui odiando, sin saberlo.

Llegó a ser una reina,
fastuosa de tesoros...
¡Qué iracundia de yel y sin sentido!

...Mas se fue desnudando.
Y yo le sonreía.

Se quedó con la túnica
de su inocencia antigua.
Creí de nuevo en ella.

Y se quitó la túnica,
y apareció desnuda toda...
¡Oh pasión de mi vida, poesía
desnuda, mía para siempre!

Eternidades

At first she came to me,
a maiden, dressed in her innocence.
And I loved her with the eyes of a child.

Then she started to dress
with all sorts of fancy attire.
And I started to hate her, not knowing why.

She became a queen,
magnificent in her jewellery...
What senseless wrath, what bitterness!

She began undressing.
And I smiled at her.

All that was left was the gown
of her former innocence.
I believed in her again.

Finally, she took off her gown too,
and appeared in her nakedness...
Oh naked poetry, passion of my life
and now forever mine!

By J. Segura, Puerta del Sol, 4, Madrid

El dormir es como un puente
que va del hoy al mañana.
Por debajo, como un sueño,
pasa el agua.

Eternidades

* * * * *

Sleeping is like a bridge
which spans today and tomorrow.
Underneath, like a dream,
the water flows by.

MADRUGADA

El amanecer tiene
esa tristeza de llegar,
en tren, a una estación que no es la de uno.

¡Qué agrios los rumores
de un día que se sabe pasajero
– oh vida mía! –

– Arriba, con el alba, llora un niño –.

Eternidades

DAWN

Daybreak has
that sad sense of arriving,
by train, to someone else's destination.

How bitter the sounds of voices
of a day, we know, can't last forever
– oh my life! –

High up, with the dawn, a child's cry...

¡No corras, ve despacio,
que adonde tienes que ir es a ti solo!

¡Ve despacio, no corras,
que el niño de tu yo, reciennacido
eterno,
no te puede seguir!

Eternidades

Don't run, go slowly
as your destination is yourself!

Go slowly, don't run,
for the child in yourself, just born
and always part of you,
cannot follow you!

WEDDING PHOTOGRAPH

Ante mí estás, sí.
Mas me olvido de ti,
pensando en ti.

Eternidades

* * * * *

Before me you are, you are.
But I forget you
thinking of you.

35

A DANTE

(...Allegro sí, che appena il conoscia...
                                    DANTE)

Tu soneto, lo mismo
que una mujer desnuda y casta,
sentándome en sus piernas puras,
me abrazó con sus brazos celestiales.

Soñé, después, con él, con ella.
                    Era una fuente
que dos chorros arqueaba en una taza
primera, la cual, luego, los vertía,
finos, en otras dos...

Eternidades

TO DANTE

(…Allegro sí, che appena il conoscia…
                                        DANTE)

Your sonnet,
like a chaste and naked woman,
taking me on her innocent knees,
embraced me with celestial arms.

Then I dreamt of it, and of her.
                    There was a fountain
with two arching jets streaming into a basin
and then, out of it, two fine springs,
pouring…

Yo no soy yo.

    Soy éste
que va a mi lado sin yo verlo;
que, a veces, voy a ver,
y que, a veces, olvido.
El que calla, sereno, cuando hablo,
el que perdona, dulce, cuando odio,
el que pasea por donde no estoy,
el que quedará en pie cuando yo muera.

Eternidades

38

I am not me.

       I am he,
who walks at my side without my seeing him;
who, at times, I am aware of,
who, at times, I forget.
He, who is silent, peaceful, when I speak;
he, who pardons gently, when I hate;
he, who can tread where I am not,
he, who will still live on when I am gone.

Soy como un niño distraído,
que arrastran de la mano
por la fiesta del mundo.
Los ojos se me cuelgan, tristes,
de las cosas...
¡Y qué dolor cuando me tiran de ellos!

Eternidades

I am like an absent-minded child
who is being dragged by the hand
through the fiesta of the world.
My eyes cling, sadly,
to things…
And how it hurts when they tear me away from them!

Piedra y Cielo
(1917–1918)

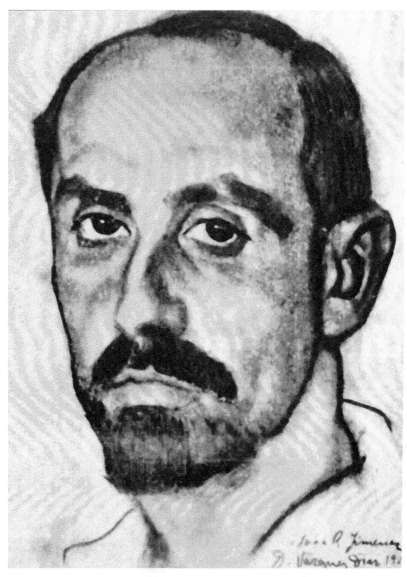

Drawing by Daniel Vázquez Díaz (Madrid, 1917)

EL POEMA

¡No le toques ya más,
que así es la rosa!

Piedra y cielo

* * * * *

POEM

Do not touch it any more
for the rose is just that!

EL RECUERDO

El río pasa por debajo
de mi alma, socavándome.
Apenas me mantengo
en mí. No me sostiene
el cielo. Las estrellas
me engañan; no, no están
arriba, sino abajo, allá en el fondo...

¿Soy? ¡Seré!
Seré, hecho onda
del río del recuerdo...

¡Contigo, agua corriente!

Piedra y cielo

MEMORIES

A river is flowing in the depths
of my soul, undermining me.
I find it very difficult
to go on. Heaven
doesn't help. Even the stars
deceive me; no stars are there
above me, only down there in the depths...

Am I? I will be!
I will be, a ripple
on the river of memory ...

Running water, I shall be with you!

MARES

¡Siento que el barco mío
ha tropezado, allá en el fondo,
con algo grande!

¡Y nada
sucede! Nada... Quietud... Olas...

— ¿Nada sucede; o es que ha sucedido todo,
y estamos ya, tranquilos, en lo nuevo? —

Piedra y cielo

SEAS

I feel this ship of mine
has struck, down in the depths,
against something vast!

And nothing
happens! Nothing... All still... Waves...

– Nothing happens? Or has everything happened
and we are now, tranquil, within the new?

NOCTURNO SOÑADO

La tierra lleva por la tierra;
mas tú, mar,
llevas por el cielo.

¡Con qué seguridad de luz de plata y oro,
nos marcan las estrellas
la ruta! – Se diría
que es la tierra el camino
del cuerpo,
que el mar es el camino
del alma –.

Sí, parece
que es el alma la sola viajera
del mar; que el cuerpo, solo,
se quedó allá en las playas,
sin ella, despidiéndola,
pesado, frío, igual que muerto.

¡Qué semejante
el viaje del mar al de la muerte,
al de la eterna vida!

Piedra y cielo

DREAM NOCTURNE

The earth leads through the earth;
but you sea,
you lead through heaven.

With what assurance, – oh, gold and silver light! –
the stars mark out
the way for us! – It could be said
that the earth is the way
of the body,
that the sea is the way
of the soul –

Yes, it seems
that the soul is the lone traveller
of the sea; that the body, alone,
is left behind on the shore,
without her, bidding her farewell,
heavy and cold, as if dead.

How similar
is the sea voyage to death,
to eternal life!

EPITAFIO IDEAL
DE UN MARINERO

Hay que buscar, para saber
tu tumba, por el firmamento.
– Llueve tu muerte de una estrella.
La losa no te pesa, que es un universo
de ensueño –.
En la ignorancia, estás
en todo – cielo, mar y tierra – muerto.

Piedra y cielo

IDEAL EPITAPH
FOR A SAILOR

We must look in the firmament
to find your grave.
– Your death rains down from a star.
The stone does not lie heavy on you, it is a universe
of dreams –
Unaware, you dwell
in everything – in heaven, sea and earth – a dead man.

¡Quisiera que mi libro
fuese, como es el cielo por la noche,
todo verdad presente, sin historia!

Que, como él, se diera en cada instante,
todo, con todas sus estrellas; sin
que niñez, juventud, vejez quitaran
ni pusieran encanto a su hermosura inmensa.

¡Temblor, relumbre, música
presentes y totales!
¡Temblor, relumbre, música en la frente
– cielo del corazón – del libro puro!

Piedra y cielo

Would that my book
could be as the sky at night,
full of actual truth – without history.

That, like the sky, it would always reveal
all things, with all their stars; neither
childhood, nor youth, nor old age could take away
or add charm to their endless beauty.

Actual and fulfilling music,
brightness, earth tremor!
Tremor, brightness, music in my mind
– sky of the heart – of the chaste book!

Poesía
(en Verso)
(1917–1923)

Belleza
(en Verso)
(1917–1923)

Dejad las puertas abiertas
esta noche, por si él
quiere, esta noche, venir,
que está muerto.

        Abierto todo,
a ver si nos parecemos
a su cuerpo; a ver si somos
algo de su alma, estando
entregados al espacio;
a ver si el gran infinito
nos echa un poco, invadiéndonos,
de nosotros; si morimos
un poco aquí; y allí, en él,
vivimos un poco.

        ¡Abierta
toda la casa, lo mismo
que si estuviera de cuerpo
presente en la noche azul,
con nosotros como sangre,
con las estrellas por flores!

Poesía (en verso)

Leave the doors open
tonight, just in case
he, who is dead, wishes
to come in.

Let's open everything
to see if we resemble
his body; to see if we are
some part of his soul, being
surrendered to space;
to see if the great infinite,
by invading us, casts
a little out of ourselves; if we die
a little here and there, in him,
we live a little.

Let
all the house be open, just as if
his body were laid out
in the blue night,
with us like blood,
with the stars for flowers!

¿Cómo, muerte, tenerte
miedo? ¿No estás aquí conmigo, trabajando?
¿No te toco en mis ojos; no me dices
que no sabes de nada, que eres hueca,
inconciente y pacífica? ¿No gozas,
conmigo, todo: gloria, soledad,
amor, hasta tus tuétanos?
¿No me estás aguantando,
muerte, de pie, la vida?
¿No te traigo y te llevo, ciega,
como tu lazarillo? ¿No repites
con tu boca pasiva
lo que quiero que digas? ¿No soportas,
esclava, la bondad con que te obligo?
¿Qué verás, qué dirás, adónde irás
sin mí? ¿No seré yo,
muerte, tu muerte, a quien tú, muerte,
debes temer, mimar, amar?

Poesía (en verso)

60

Death, how can I be afraid of you?
Are you not beside me working?
Do I not touch you with my eyes; do you not tell me
that you know nothing, that you are hollow,
unconscious and peaceful? Do you not enjoy
everything with me: fame, loneliness,
love, through and through, to the marrow of your bones?
Are you not standing here,
Death, enduring life with me?
Do I not lead you up and down, blind Death,
like your blindman's guide? Do you not repeat
with your passive lips
what I want you to say? Do you not suffer,
slave, from my compelling kindness?
What will you see or say, where will you go
without me? Will not I be, Death,
your death, whom you, Death,
must fear, pamper and love?

EL SOLO AMIGO

No me alcanzarás, amigo.
Llegarás ansioso, loco;
pero yo me habré ya ido.

– ¡Y qué espantoso vacío
todo lo que yo haya puesto
detrás por venir conmigo!

¡Y qué lamentable abismo
todo lo que yo haya puesto
en medio, sin culpa, amigo! –

No podrás quedarte, amigo…
Yo quizás volveré al mundo;
pero tú ya te habrás ido.

Poesía (en verso)

THE ONLY FRIEND

You will not reach me, my friend.
You will arrive full of anxiety, going mad,
but I will have already left.

And what a dreadful emptiness,
all that I have left behind
to follow my true self!

And what a wailing abyss,
all that I have placed
between us, through no fault of mine, friend!

You will not be able to stay, dear friend ...
Perhaps I shall return to the world;
but you will have already left.

MADRE

¿Todo acabado, todo,
el mirar, la sonrisa;
todo, hasta lo más leve
de lo más grande?

¡No, yo sé, madre mía,
que tú, nada inmortal, un día eterno,
seguirás sonriéndome, mirándome
a mí, nada infinita!

Poesía (en verso)

MOTHER

Has all ended, all,
the gaze, the smile;
all, even what is slightest
in what is greatest?

No, dear mother, I know
that you, immortal nothingness, everlasting day,
will always be smiling, looking
on me, infinite nothingness!

Juan Ramón Jiménez in 1949

MADRE

¡Si pudiera llevarte
yo a la nada, en mis brazos, de tu vida,
como tú me llevabas, cuando niño,
de tu pecho a la cuna!

Belleza (en verso)

* * * * *

MOTHER

I wish I could carry you,
in my arms, from your life to nothingness,
as you would carry me, as a baby,
from your bosom to the cradle!

CENIT

Yo no seré yo, muerte,
hasta que tú te unas con mi vida
y me completes así todo:
hasta que mi mitad de luz se cierre
con mi mitad de sombra
– y sea yo equilibrio eterno
en la mente del mundo:
unas veces, mi medio yo, radiante:
otras, mi otro medio yo, en olvido –.

Yo no seré yo, muerte,
hasta que tú, en tu turno, vistas
de huesos pálidos mi alma.

Belleza (en verso)

ZENITH

I shall not be, oh death,
until you come to join my life
and in this way make me whole;
until my half-light becomes one
with my half-shadow
– and I might reach the eternal balance
within the world's mind:
at times one half of me, radiant;
at times my other half, in oblivion –

I will not be, oh death,
until you, when your time comes,
dress my soul in pale bones.

La Estación Total
(Canciones de la Nueva Luz)
(1923–1936)

RENACERÉ YO

Renaceré yo piedra,
y aún te amaré mujer a ti.

Renaceré yo viento,
y aún te amaré mujer a ti.

Renaceré yo ola,
y aún te amaré mujer a ti.

Renaceré yo fuego,
y aún te amaré mujer a ti.

Renaceré yo hombre,
y aún te amaré mujer a ti.

La estación total
(Canciones de la nueva luz)

I SHALL BE REBORN

I shall be reborn a stone,
and woman I shall still love you.

I shall be reborn as the wind,
and woman I shall still love you.

I shall be reborn a wave,
and woman I shall still love you.

I shall be reborn as fire,
and woman I shall still love you.

I shall be reborn a man,
and woman I shall still love you.

TU DESNUDEZ

La rosa:
tu desnudez hecha gracia.

La fuente:
tu desnudez hecha agua.

La estrella:
tu desnudez hecha alma.

La estación total
(Canciones de la nueva luz)

YOUR NAKEDNESS

Rose:
your nakedness, made grace.

Fountain:
your nakedness, made water.

Star:
your nakedness, made soul.

LUZ TÚ

Luz vertical
luz tú;
alta luz tú,
luz oro;
luz vibrante,
luz tú.

Y yo la negra, ciega, sorda, muda sombra horizontal.

La estación total
(Canciones de la nueva luz)

YOU LIGHT

Vertical light,
you light;
lofty light,
you, golden light,
vibrant light,
you light.

And I the black, the blind, the deaf, the dumb horizontal shadow.

CHRONOLOGY

1881	Juan Ramón Jiménez was born on the 23rd December in Moguer (Huelva). His father, Victor Jiménez, was Castilian and his mother, Purificación Mantecón, was Andalucian.
1893	He began to study in the Jesuit public school of San Luis Gonzaga, in the port of Santa María (Cádiz).
1896	After graduating from his Junior College in autumn, he began to study Law at Seville University. He also studied painting in the studio of Salvador Clemente and read Bécquer.
1898	He abandoned his studies and returned ill to Moguer after his father suffered a heart attack.
1900	He arrived in Madrid in April after accepting an invitation by Rubén Darío and Francisco Villaespesa. The death of his father triggered a serious psychological illness. This preoccupation with death lasted the rest of his life.
1901	Following the advice of the family doctor in Moguer, J.R.J. was committed into La Maison de Santé du Castel d'Andorte, near Bordeaux. In September he returned to Madrid and was admitted into the Rosario Sanatorium through the intercession of Dr. Simarro.
1903	He started to live in the house of Dr. Simarro. A friendship began with Giner de los Ríos and members of the Free Teaching Institution.
1906	Back in Moguer, he spent a period of isolation and solitude, with visits to the cemetery, painting and reading.
1911	With the ruin of his family, the Bank of Spain repossessed his family's estate. Publication of *La soledad sonora* and *Poemas májicos y dolientes* (Lib. de F. Fe.)
1912	In December he returned to Madrid.

1913	He met and fell in love with Zenobia Camprubí. He moved into the Residencia de Estudiantes.
1914	Publication of the first edition of *Platero y yo*. J.R.J. began to help Zenobia with the translation, from English to Castilian, of the works of Rabindranath Tagore. His health improved.
1916	J.R.J. travelled to New York. On the 2nd March he married Zenobia in the church of Saint Stephen.
1917	Publication of the complete edition of *Platero y yo*, *Sonetos espirituales* and *Diario de un poeta recién casado*, which began to show his distinctive spelling. The Hispanic Society in New York published *Poesías escogidas*.
1918	Publication of *Eternidades*. (A. de Angel, Alcoy). Eternidades marked a new direction in J.R.J.'s writing.
1919	Publication of *Piedra y cielo* (Ed. Fortanet).
1922	Publication of *La segunda antolojía poética* (1898–1918), (Ed. Espasa Calpe).
1923	Publication of *Poesía* and *Belleza*, edited by J.R.J. & Zenobia (Ed. Poligráficos).
1928	Deaths of the mother of Zenobia on 18th August and of the mother of J.R.J. on the 1st September.
1931	J.R.J. celebrated the proclamation of the Spanish Republic enthusiastically. The tumour that would end the life of Zenobia appeared.
1932	Publication of the anthology *Poesía en prosa y verso* (1902 – 1932), (Ed. Signo).
1934	He met Gabriela Mistral.
1936	On the 18th July the uprising against the Constitutional Government broke out. The president Azaña appointed J.R.J. as Honorary Cultural Attaché to the United States. J.R.J. and Zenobia began a campaign of support for the Republic. Trip to Puerto Rico and Cuba.
1937–1938	Declarations and acts of support for the Republic.

1939	The Civil War ended on the 1st April with the triumph of the Franco's troops. J.R.J. started to help the intellectuals exiled in France. Losing hope of a return to Spain, and with an acute nervous breakdown, Zenobia and J.R.J. moved to the university district of Miami.
1940	Suffering from a serious depression, J.R.J. had to be hospitalised.
1942	Publication of *Españoles de tres mundos*, (Ed. Losada, Buenos Aires) a book of prose about his contemporaries.
1945	Zenobia appointed professor in Maryland. J.R.J. did not accept the offer of Don José María Pemán of his candidature to the Spanish Royal Academy of Language. They moved to Riverdale to be near to the University.
1946	Publication of *La estación total*, (Ed. Losada, Buenos Aires). Intense depression.
1949	Publication of *Animal de fondo*, (Ed. Pleamar, Buenos Aires).
1950	Due to his serious depression doctors advised him to go to a Spanish-speaking place. He travelled to Puerto Rico.
1951	Zenobia abandoned her work in Maryland and established her residency in Puerto Rico. Zenobia's old tumour degenerated into cancer.
1952	With an improvement of his nervous condition, J.R.J. returned to give conferences and review his work.
1954	The illness of Zenobia deteriorated and with that, the depression of J.R.J.
1955	The Zenobia-Juan Ramón Room was opened in the library of the University of Puerto Rico. Large donation of manuscripts, books, paintings and personal letters. The Zenobia y Juan Ramón Municipal House of Culture was created in Moguer. Faced with the worsening of Zenobia, J.R.J. was struck with a serious depression.
1956	The University of Maryland, supported by other Universities, official entities and individuals from the United States, proposed the candidature of J.R.J. for the Nobel Prize for

Literature. On the 25th October J.R.J. received the telegram announcing the concession of the Prize. Zenobia died three days later of vaginal cancer.

1957   J.R.J. confined himself to his house. Thanks to the collaboration of Don Eugenio Florit he published *Tercera antolojía poética* (1898 – 1953), (Ed. Bib. Nueva). The personal archive of J.R.J. was moved to the Zenobia-Juan Ramón Room.

1958   After suffering a fall and fracturing his hip, he became ill with bronchopneumonia on the 28th of May and he died in the early hours of the morning on the 29th of May. Thanks to the negotiations of his nephew, Don Francisco Hernández-Pinzón, the mortal remains of Zenobia and Juan Ramón received burial in the cemetery in Moguer underneath the clear blue sky.

* * * * * * * *

To Juan Ramón Jiménez

He has other gardens. Jasmine
longs for summer's fairs,
and these scented lyres,
sweet lyres plucked by the cool wind.

Antonio Machado

BIBLIOGRAPHY

Alarcón Sierra, R., *Juan Ramón Jiménez. Poesía perfecta,* Espasa Calpe, Madrid, 2003.

Alberti, R., *Introduzione a poesie,* Newton Compton, Roma, 1971.

Albornoz, A. de, (ed.), *Juan Ramón Jiménez,* Taurus, Madrid, 1981.

Albornoz, A. de, (ed.), *Nueva antología, Península,* Barcelona, 1981.

Albornoz, A. de, (ed.), *Espacio,* Editora Nacional, Madrid, 1982.

Blasco, F.J., (ed.) *Selección de prosa lírica,* Espasa Calpe, Madrid, 1990.

Bo, C., *La poesía con Juan Ramón,* Florencia, Edizioni di Rivoluzioni, 1941.

Caballero, A., *Prólogo a libros de poesía de J.R.J.,* Aguilar, Madrid, 1957.

Campoamor González, A., *Bibliografía general de Juan Ramón Jiménez,* Taurus, Madrid 1983.

Campoamor González, A., *Vida y poesía de Juan Ramón Jiménez,* Sedmay, Madrid, 1976.

Campoamor González, A., *Bibliografía de Juan Ramón Jiménez,* Fundación Juan Ramón Jiménez, Huelva, 2000.

Camprubí, Z., *Juan Ramón y yo,* Ayuntamiento de Moguer, Moguer, 1987.

Camprubí, Z., *Vivir con Juan Ramón,* ed. de Arturo del Villar, Los Libros de Fausto, Madrid, 1986.

Cano, J.L., *Poesía española del siglo XX,* Guadarrama, Madrid, 1960.

Cernuda, L., *Estudios sobre poesía española contemporánea,* Guadarrama, Madrid, 1957.

Champourcín, E., *La ardilla y la rosa (Juan Ramón en mi memoria),* Fundación Juan Ramón Jiménez, Moguer, 1996.

Dennis, N., *Perfume and poison. A study of the relationship between José Bergamín and Juan Ramón Jiménez,* Reichenberger, Kassel, 1985.

Díaz-Plaja, G., *J.R.J. en su poesía,* Aguilar, Madrid, 1958.

Díaz-Plaja, G., *La poesía lírica española,* Labor, Barcelona, 1937.

Diego, G., (ed.), *Poesía española contemporánea,* Taurus, Madrid, 1959.

Díez Canedo, E, *J.R.J. en su obra,* El Colegio de México, México, 1944.

Figueira, G., *J.R.J. poeta de lo inefable,* Biblioteca Alfar, Montevideo, 1944.

Fogelquist, D.F., *J.R.J. vida y obra,* Hispanic Institute, New York, 1958.

Fogelquist, D.F., *Juan Ramón Jiménez,* Twayne, Boston, 1976.

Friedrich, H., *Die Struktur der modernen Lyrik,* Rowohlt Taschenbuch, Hamburg, 1956.

Garfias, F., *Juan Ramón Jiménez*, Taurus, Madrid, 1958.

Garfias, F., *Prólogo a primeros libros de poesía de J.R.J.*, Aguilar, Madrid, 1959.

Gómez de la Serna, R., *Retratos contemporáneos*, Sudamericana, Buenos Aires, 1941. (Aguilar, Madrid, 1989).

González Villegas, M., *Leyendo a J.R.J.*, Gaceta Comercial, Montevideo,1949.

Guerrero Ruiz, J., *Juan Ramón de viva voz*, Insula, Madrid, 1961.

Gullón, R., *Conversaciones con J.R.J.*, Taurus, Madrid, 1958.

Gullón, R., *Monumento de amor (Cartas de Zenobia Camprubí y Juan Ramón Jiménez)*, Ediciones de la Torre, Universidad de Puerto Rico, San Juan, 1959.

Gullón, R., *Relaciones entre Antonio Machado y J.R.J.*, Università di Pisa, Pisa, 1964.

Hernández-Pinzón Jiménez, F., *Zenobia y Juan Ramón en la trágica gloria del Premio Nobel*, Artes Gráficas Luis Pérez, Madrid. 1971.

Neddermann, E., *Die Symbolistischen Stilemente im Werke von J.R.J.*, Seminar für Romanische Sprachen und Kultur, Hamburg, 1935.

Owre, J.R., *Juan Ramón Jiménez and Zenobia. Their association with the University of Miami*, The Carrel, University of Miami, 8, 2 (1967), pp. 1–4.

Palau de Nemes, G., *Vida y obra de Juan Ramón Jiménez. La poesía desnuda*, Gredos, Madrid, 1974.

Palau de Nemes, G., *Vida y obra de Juan Ramón Jiménez*, Gredos, Madrid, 1957.

Predmore, M.P., *La obra en prosa de Juan Ramón Jiménez*. Gredos, Madrid, 1966.

Predmore, M.P., *La poesía hermética de Juan Ramón Jiménez*, Gredos, Madrid, 1973.

Salinas, P., *Literatura española: siglo XX*, Séneca, México, 1941.

Sánchez-Barbudo, A., *La segunda época de J.R.J. (1916–1953)*, Gredos, Madrid, 1962.

Trend, J.B., *Fifty Spanish Poems*, University of California Press, Berkeley, 1951.

Vitier, C., (ed.), *Juan Ramón Jiménez en Cuba*, Editorial Arte y Literatura, La Habana, 1981.

Printed and bound by CPI Group (UK) Ltd, Croydon, CR0 4YY

13/04/2025

14656593-0002